Sounds of Morning

poems by

Anita S. Pulier

Finishing Line Press
Georgetown, Kentucky

Sounds of Morning

Copyright © 2017 by Anita S. Pulier
ISBN 978-1-63534-163-8 First Edition
All rights reserved under International and Pan-American Copyright Conventions. No part of this book may be reproduced in any manner whatsoever without written permission from the publisher, except in the case of brief quotations embodied in critical articles and reviews.

ACKNOWLEDGMENTS

Askew: "The Razzle-Dazzle of a Long Marriage".
Buddhist Poetry Review: "One Poet Too Many".
Cultural Weekly: "House Poet Wanted", "Knit One Purl Two", "Sounds of Morning".
Grabbing the Apple: "Feng Shui in 13E".
Riverbabble: "One Poet Too Many".
Your Daily Poem: "Aubade", "Metropolitan Farming", "Pruning", "She Says".

Publisher: Leah Maines

Editor: Christen Kincaid

Cover Art and Design: Myron Pulier

Author Photo: Myron Pulier

Printed in the USA on acid-free paper.
Order online: www.finishinglinepress.com
also available on amazon.com

Author inquiries and mail orders:
Finishing Line Press
P. O. Box 1626
Georgetown, Kentucky 40324
U. S. A.

Table of Contents

House Poet Wanted 1
Aubade 2
One Poet Too Many 3
Feng Shui in 13E 4
Sounds of Morning 6
Playing Along 8
Metropolitan Farming 9
Safe Harbor 10
She Says 11
Party of One 12
Caution! 13
Hip Hip 14
Morning e-mail 15
The Razzle-Dazzle of a Long Marriage 16
The 9th Planet 17
Define Hapless 18
Pruning 19
An Insomniac's Dream Brain 20
Housekeeping 21
Boots 22
Eclipse 23
Knit One Purl Two 25
Keys 27
Sharing the Lie 28

To Jake, Will, Chloe, Georgia and Lily… living poetry.

House Poet Wanted

Experienced, articulate,
references required.
Job requires weaving
the fibers of household matter
and daily routines into an examined life.
Must explain the dagger through the heart,
the nail piercing the skull,
memories triggered by the scent
of Mama's over-salted soup.
Applicant must define the life worth living,
identify ancestors stuck together
in that box of sepia photos,
be plain spoken, persistent,
willing to be misunderstood,
interpreted to death.

Aubade

In the shade-crackled light of early morning
I am lifted into the fabric of the day
ready to hear the sharp-edged songbirds
orchestrating yet another welcome prelude.

A surge of energy ties loose ends,
offers reason to rise from deepest sleep
and plunge into the icy mix.

Beyond the children born,
beyond a lifelong partner at my side,
beyond the songbirds' incessant chatter,

I wake surrounded by many selves
each of whom
I am still learning to embrace
at the start of day.

One Poet Too Many

In the dank underground passage
between the L train and the 3
New Yorkers race East and West.

Midway,
tattered hand lettered signs
taped to cinderblock walls announce:

I write poems.
I am a NY Times published poet.
I will write a poem to order.

Crumpled on the ground is the poet,
a fortress of ragged clothes
surrounds him as he sleeps.
Commuters rush by,
not one wakes him to order a poem.

The rush hour hordes
move in waves like schools of fish.

In the dim tunnel light,
to a wounded poet,
we may actually seem connected.

Feng Shui in 13E

I am feeling reckless,
reading Kerouac,
studying *Feng Shui*,
leaving the toilet seat cover up

in an attempt
to allow bad Qi to escape
through NYC sewers.

Cannot recall
when I last cleaned the bowl.
Even the worst of Qi
may refuse my offer.

After checking
that the doorman is on duty
I open wide the front door.

Qi wafts through 13E
delighted with the absence
of locks and chains.

I run the water in the bathtub
creating a trickling fountain
check my image in the

mirror now reflecting a
babbling brook, move furniture,
begin to understand the art

of relationships,
connectivity,
toilets, open doors,

water and reflecting mirrors,
all rearranged,
setting the stage
for absolute bliss.

Then... nothing.
I hold vigil for the arrival
of inner peace.

Ambulance sirens scream,
neighbors shout,
children cry, dogs bark.

I watch you trip over the chair
I have just moved to allow
for the free movement of Qi.

While you curse,
I move the chair back,
turn off the water in the tub, re-chain the front door,

hope that Qi will forgive me,
allow me to get on with
muddling through,

an ancient art
I have spent years perfecting.

Sounds of Morning

Sleep has infused
his brain with energy
transformed into words.

I watch his mouth moving,
his disheveled silvery hair,
his familiar faraway look.

I try to stay focused
while he lectures
on theories of black holes,

the ninth planet,
evolutionary development,
how the brain works

religion, politics,
and ultimately,
solutions, not always pretty.
Squinting in the pale light
of early morning
I silently review our numbers,

years behind,
years ahead,

Our feet touch,
rustle the sheets
as he decodes

the puzzle
of the very earth
I simply tread upon.

I used to wonder why
he shares these
early morning rambles with

a woman who hasn't
read a science book since sixth grade
until one morning

he pauses and says, *Say something.*
I raise my eyebrows, ask, *Why?*
I like hearing your voice, he says, tenderly.

Playing Along

The orchid arrived
swaddled in celebratory paper,
two curved stems balletically
balancing six improbable
naked blooms.

I, no youngster,
knew this might not end well.

Still, I played along,
placed the shameless display
near a gritty window,
watered the mossy base,
allowed sunlight
to ooze through the slats
of a dusty venetian blind,
invited light to invade
helter-skelter, fearlessly
nurturing extraordinary beauty
despite the lousy odds.

Metropolitan Farming

First the bulbs from a third grade
school catalog that quietly
died in their cracked coffee cup,

then, propped on toothpicks,
the avocado pit
stretching its desperate roots

into stale water before
bidding farewell to the disgruntled potato,
too busy rotting to notice,

next came the goldfish and hamsters,
showered with attention and treats
until they too keeled over.

And so we taught
our city children responsibility,
the wonder of life-giving forces,
how to cope with disappointment,

the art of pushing on.

Safe Harbor
> *At the end of the day, you can only be from one place.*
> *The mind needs a geographical harbor.*
> —Isabelle Dupuy

Like the boy raised by wolves
we have our own language
our own compass, our own

calendar worthy
of academic study,
divisions have blurred,

weeks into months,
years flit by on hackneyed wing,
impossible for the most astute
scientist to isolate one day,

devise a celebration
for that which cannot be
described or explained
by the clichés of ordinary time,

until in the middle of the night
you whisper a few words in my ear
in an ancient language and patiently
listen as I respond.

She Says

He says and she says and then I says
    the girl holds her phone aloft
ear plugs dangle from each side of her frazzled head
    a tiny microphone suspended in mid air
and then I says and she says and can you believe
    what he says
undaunted by honking horns and screaming sirens
and then he says and then she says and
    can you guess what I says
embracing the great tradition of oral storytelling
this gum cracking adolescent avoids the pitfall of
    past or future tenses
and with the wisdom of Buddha stays rooted in
    the present moment
assuming that it will last long enough to get her
    wherever she is going

Party of One

In the silent murky air
of a sleepless night
I surrender to failure,
curl knobby toes
on cool kitchen tile,
bite into a perfect
end of summer peach,
celebrate the inevitable.

Caution!

If you are puffed up pleased
or peacock proud—
play it safe,
knock on wood.

If the path is dark
and strange noises
bounce off the winding road—
take no chances,
spit over your left shoulder.

Neither courage nor reason
can offer this brand of comfort.

Sure, question everything,
but why miss even
the smallest chance to tame
the untamable,

assuage spirits,
keep the plane aloft,
the car filled with teenagers safe.

Still, I know no way
to cancel the curse
of the silky black cat who
time and again crosses my path,

taunting, leaving
me immobile, stunned,
besotted by its charm.

Hip Hip

Internal secrets
lugged everywhere,
anatomical baggage.

Each step a complex
ball and socket rotation
never taught, never learned,

yet flawlessly performed
navigating the rugged earth
with the ease of an Olympian.

Until an unfathomable
concoction of bone and cartilage
incites a protest

as hungry muscles
extinguish Automatic,
reset controls to Manual,

exhibit no empathy,
display no guidelines,
hit or miss, balance or topple.

The timing is stunning
an "I" poem escapes
attempts in verse

to jettison a lifetime of stiff upper lips,
replace the abstract
with the unwelcome concrete,

while chowing down
a tasteless diet
of resignation.

Morning e-mail

Every morning I get an e-mail from Canada
offering me a larger penis.
Canada? Land of the Royal Mounties?
Sixties haven for conscientious objectors, Canada?

Now, so many years between today and the 60s,
pressed to accept frailty, acknowledge fragility,
there may be a few things I would pay northern strangers
for, but Alas Dear Canada, a larger penis is not one of them.

Perhaps a better more efficient way
for aging partners to make it through the night
in spoon contour, without a single fruitless
adjustment to aching parts,

or an easy to swallow capsule
to soothe jagged nerves,
restoring them and the weary muscles
to which they attach, to youthful elasticity,

Or a moment of comfort,
I might pay for a moment of comfort,
against the terrifying silence
of a long sleepless night.

The Razzle-Dazzle of a Long Marriage

The Truth must dazzle gradually.
—*Emily Dickinson*

Okay Emily,
I will hint,
scatter clues

hidden in
metaphors
about long durable couplings.

It races by
him, elusive,
teasing, indefinable.

Squinting in its
glaring light, frustrated,
I fight the temptation to leave it and him to stew.

But when he adoringly barks,
Stop, come back,
why can't you just say it?

I am the one dazzled and turn back,
recalculate, celebrate our glorious
unfettered *It*.

The 9th Planet
> *Pluto, at its most distant, is 4.6 billion miles from the sun....*
> *One trip around the sun would take 10,000 to 20,000 years.*
> —NY Times Jan. 20, 2016

That little telescope collecting dust
in the attic
is now set up on our roof.

I tilt my head towards the sky,
on high alert for
an unexpected universe

and the ultimate swap:
that which has been defined
for that with no boundaries.

The evangelicals are
outside my window
keening to the worried sky.

Look, I say sweetly,
don't panic, this 9th planet
will orbit every 20,000 years.

I trust you'll
have time to adjust.

Define Hapless

> *Suspected Burglar Gets Stuck In Chimney,*
> *Dies After Fire Is Lit.*
> —*Huffington Post, Nov. 29, 2015*

Lodged,
emitting animal noises.
Skin, stripped by rough brick
scrapes off in bloody bits.
Swollen mass jammed
between sky and hearth.

Moonlight and blinking stars,
provide tomb light,
soaring birds tweet,
soft drizzle moistens
two buggy eyes.
Flames lick rag doll limbs.

The future, the past,
good fortune and despair
ghost the fresh corpse.

Pruning

> *To be astonished is one of the surest*
> *ways of not growing old too quickly.*
> —Colette

Patio gardener,
I know so little about nature.
Water and snip,
eliminate stragglers.
If dumb luck prevails
new shoots push up
through soil jammed
into little pots.
Odd, the excitement
watching tiny sprouts
redefine old.
This is where it gets
complicated.
Nota bene: I may
feel astonished
but choose to tip my hat
to the here and now,
sort the garbage
turn off the kitchen lights
move into sunlight, squint to
read the directions
on supermarket plant food,
place a teaspoon of the
magical blue powder
in the battered watering can,
celebrate renewal.

An Insomniac's Dream Brain

> *My job as a writer is mainly to edit the creative rush.*
> *The dream brain is the creative engine.*
> —Russell Edson

The dream brain demands much
from its sleepless servants
riding the rip tide of daily cycles,

insisting on celebrating in broad
daylight when rem
has held itself at bay,

sporting a devilish grin
as the bleary eyed slump
at disordered desks desperate to

trap an errant rush. In the haze
of rapid eye movement deficits
the dream brain trifles with historical facts

flirts with memory
teases the weary
as they tap keyboards.

Fully awake, those very words,
positively brilliant in a dream brain trance,
appear ridiculous,

stranding innocent insomniacs
in the webby space between sleep
and exhaustion with no options left but

to wait for the perfect starry night to
harness art.

Housekeeping

> *Art washes away from the soul*
> *the dust of everyday life.*
> —Pablo Picasso

Sticky, thick and ephemeral,
sweep, dust, vacuum.
We remain coated in it.

Dig, toss, catch
a flash of insight from
A stranger's right-brain.

Transform the ordinary into
something indefinable,
something stunning,
something you may regret,

something that
once exposed
refuses denial.

Boots
    For Toni

I worry about your feet.
The gritty New York snow quickly turns to slush.
I am far away but I see you walking across Central Park
    in flip flops.
Have Mt. Sinai's ICU nurses told your son that
    his Mom's feet
are wet, her toes cramped and cold?
What are the boundaries to lifelong friendships?
Whose son is in that bed?
If I ask nicely would the ICU nurses put boots on him?
I would explain that it is snowing hard, a blizzard really,
and that boots may keep him safe.

Eclipse

I assumed the world was frayed
and old, easily ignored
moons and suns hanging
in clouds of industrial air,

nodded politely
at talk of light years and
black holes,
but not today.

Today, they woke me
at 4 and here I am in
a dark deserted park

because long ago
someone on a distant hill
far from city lights,

someone with a telescope,
learned beard and
razor eyes,

lined up shadows,
arcs, computed trajectories,
all of which predicted
this very dawn,
this very minute,

when layered in sweatshirts
we would huddle for warmth,
wait for the earth to throw
a resolute shadow,

watch the light
of the sun refuse
comfort to the moon,

all while humming
an old Cat Stevens song
about Moon Shadows

as a tow headed boy,
and his gray bearded Papa
light the moment with
sky-chatter.

Knit One Purl Two
For Sima

You get a call
your brother died.

You retreat, bury yourself
under a fluff of blankets,

Tears coat your aging skin,
still dead.

You begin sharing the news with
family, friends, co-workers.

They wait for you to orchestrate
what follows dead.

You need time.
Knit one, purl two,

Maybe he will walk through that door once more
so you can be ten or twelve or fifteen

Gifting a scarf you made for him before he
left home leaving you behind,

Knit one, purl two,

The years you held close the feeling
that as long as he was somewhere, you were okay.

Now, this very minute,
you need him to be somewhere,

(Cable stitch, twist stitch)
Instead, he is dead,

You have lost count,
loose strands appear,

You pull on one
everything unravels.

You crawl out of bed
gripping a single ropey thread.

Children, grandchildren, friends call,
show up, make noise.

The thread is surprisingly elastic.
You wrap it tightly around your hand,

Your head, your spine, it moves easily
with you from bed to kitchen,

Keeps you upright,
redefines survival,

You drink juice.

Keys

Attached to an evolutionary
variety of chains
each sports a souvenir medallion,
miniature flashlight or good luck charm
jingling in every pocket and purse.

Houses, apts, bike locks, offices,
safety deposit boxes, cars
aging parents' homes, grown
children's homes, office ladies room,
gym lockers, mailboxes, diaries, lockets,
suitcases, jewelry boxes.

One by one detached and discarded
as they are rendered
useless by time,
or is it tide?
One by one
until only a few
hardy survivors remain.

Like a good sauce
boiled down to its essence,
smaller richer, more complex,
so long in the preparation
so quickly gobbled up.

Sharing the Lie

Swaddled in
hospital paraphernalia
his bony hands wave hello.

His face is covered
by an oxygen mask,
he cannot speak,

cannot explain
dying to those of us
sporting visitor passes.

We scan the scene hoping
to discover how one leaves
this messy glorious life,

flash a cardboard smile,
utter a few feeble
words say a cheery goodbye

embracing the *folie à deux*:
that we will soon
be dining out,

complaining about the service,
the overcooked food, trading stories
about kids, arguing politics.

He smiles back
giving life to
our unspoken lie.

After retiring from law practice **Anita S. Pulier** served as a U.S. representative for the Women's International League for Peace and Freedom at the United Nations. Her chapbooks *Perfect Diet* and *The Lovely Mundane* were published by Finishing Line Press. Anita's poems have appeared in many journals both online and in print.

www.ingramcontent.com/pod-product-compliance
Lightning Source LLC
LaVergne TN
LVHW041513070426
835507LV00012B/1541